CROWNED HEART SERIES — BOOK ONE

Martha Root

Written by Melanie Lotfali

Illustrated by Katayoun Mottahedin

Crowned Heart Series – Martha Root

Text © Copyright Melanie Lotfali
Illustrations © Copyright Katayoun Mottahedin
Original book design by Monib Mahdavi

First Edition 2008
Second Edition 2016
All Rights Reserved

Licensed under a Creative Commons
Attribution-NonCommercial-ShareAlike 4.0
International License

www.melanielotfali.com

hardcover ISBN 978-0-9946018-0-3
softcover ISBN 978-0-9945926-8-2

How many queens of the world have laid down their heads on a pillow of dust and disappeared… Not so the handmaids who ministered at the Threshold of God; these have shone forth like glittering stars in the skies of ancient glory, shedding their splendors across all the reaches of time.

'Abdu'l-Bahá

There are queens who wear crowns on their heads. Their crowns are made of earthly things like gold and diamonds and rubies.

And there are queens who wear crowns in their hearts. Their crowns are made of heavenly things, like love and courage and humility. This is the story about one of those queens. Her name is Martha Root.

Martha Root met 'Abdu'l-Bahá. He gave her a special and beautiful white rose.

One day 'Abdu'l-Bahá wrote some letters to His Bahá'í friends. He needed some helpers.

Martha Root wanted to become `Abdu'l-Bahá's helper.

He wanted the Bahá'ís to travel to tell people about Bahá'u'lláh. So Martha packed her suitcases. She travelled by boat over the sea…

She travelled over the mountains and she travelled through the countryside...

*S*he met kings, queens, princes and princesses. And she met people like you and me. She told them all about Bahá'u'lláh.

Sometimes she was tired or sick. Sometimes she was scared or lonely. Then Martha Root prayed. Bahá'u'lláh helped her to be strong.

Martha Root travelled all over the world. She even visited Australia! Martha Root was a true helper of 'Abdu'l-Bahá.

She made Him very happy.

The crown of Martha Root's heart is full of heavenly gems!
They shine like the sun.

Hand of the Cause of God
Martha Root

REFERENCES

The stories and facts contained in this book are from:
Harper, Barron. "*Lights of Fortitude*". August, 1997.
George Ronald, Oxford, Great Britain.

Melanie Lotfali

Melanie Lotfali PhD is a graduate of the Australian College of Journalism in Professional Writing for Children. She is the author of the Fellowship Farm series, Unity in Diversity series, and Crowned Heart series.

She currently lives in Townsville, Australia, with her family.

Katayoun Mottahedin

Katayoun Mottahedin has a Post Graduate Diploma of Education from Monash University, Bachelor of Graphic Design from Swinburne University of Technology and Diploma of Arts and Design from Chisholm Institute. Her art has been utilised in magazines, books, greeting cards, stationary and other publications.

She currently lives in Melbourne, Australia.

www.ingramcontent.com/pod-product-compliance
Lightning Source LLC
Chambersburg PA
CBHW061937290426
44113CB00025B/2945